The Yorkshire Meaning of Liff

A dictionary of things there should be words for

By Joe Moorwood

Introduced by John Lloyd CBE

Illustrated by Rowan Moorwood

The Yorkshire Meaning of Liff

A dictionary of things there should be words for

The Yorkshire Meaning of Liff twins some of the obscurely wonderful, often unheard of and wastefully under-used place names of this glorious county, with the numerous experiences, feelings, situations and objects which we all know but, for some reason, have no words attributed to them...

For the irreplaceable Matt Palmer

Great Northern Books
PO Box 213, Ilkley, LS29 9WS
www.greatnorthernbooks.co.uk

ISBN: 978-0-9576399-8-0

Design and layout: David Burrill

CIP Data
A catalogue for this book is available
from the British Library

Contents

Introduction
by John Lloyd

Most introductions don't actually introduce anyone, but this one does. May I introduce Joe Moorwood? This is now doubly odd because I don't actually *know* Joe Moorwood. We've talked for hours on the phone but never actually met.

Joe first wrote to me earlier this year, after hearing an appeal on Radio 4 for contributions to a programme called *The Meaning of Liff At 30*. Designed to mark three decades in print of a book I wrote with Douglas Adams in 1983, listeners were invited to submit new 'liffs' – definitions of 'things there should be words for' brought to life by attaching them to a place name.

Some 400 people responded to the BBC's call and the standard of entries was impressively high, but one person in particular stood out. He had not, like most contributors, come up with one or two ideas, he had written an entire book.

When this landed on my desk in February, I'm ashamed to say that I didn't open it for several weeks. After 40 years in radio and television, I think I'm right in saying I have never produced a show, directed a movie or got involved in a book based on a script sent to me out of the blue by someone I've never met. Maybe it's just me, but it's never happened yet. Until now, that is.

Because, after dutifully (and with something of a heavy heart) finally getting round to reading the manuscript, I was astonished to find myself laughing aloud. The last time anything like this occurred to me was in the mid-70s, when I was sent 11 one-liners on a piece of paper. The writer was a wonderful man called Laurie Rowley, who was then a shower-fitter from Leeds, and ten of them were genuinely hilarious.

Joe Moorwood is a fire-fighter from Sheffield – there must be something in the water up there – but he used to be in public relations. This is one of the more unusual career lurches I've come across. Did he professionally advise himself, I wonder, that 'fire-fighter' is a much cooler job description than 'PR man'? Or perhaps his office burned down one day and he took up dousing conflagrations as a kind of emergency hobby then decided it was more fun than writing press releases. I don't know, he hasn't told me yet.

After I finished his book, I called Joe straight away, and asked him if we might use some of his best definitions in *Afterliff*, the all-new 30th anniversary celebration of the original book that I was in the process of writing with another of

Douglas's old friends, Jon Canter. Joe kindly agreed and so, in that book (and in this one), you may enjoy the delights of his masterly repurposing of Fylingdales and Croome, as well as Bempton, Hampole and Norristhorpe.

Afterliff makes considerable use of liffs sent in by members of the public. Almost 200 people (about a fifth of the book) are credited, but Joe Moorwood is the uncrowned king of them all, with just under 30 definitions.

As part of our agreement, I agreed that I would try to help Joe find a market for the whole of his unaided work, and I'm delighted that the award-winning firm of Great Northern Publishing has had the perspicacity, courage and good taste to take him on.

This is the book you hold in your hands. *The Yorkshire Meaning of Liff* confines itself entirely, as you will see, to definitions of place names found in Yorkshire. This is a much harder task than we had compiling the original *The Meaning of Liff*, its successor *The Deeper Meaning of Liff* or the newly published *Afterliff*, all of which use locations from all over the world.

But this is the kind of guy Joe Moorwood is – brave, intelligent and above all seriously funny, undaunted is his middle name. Well, it probably isn't, actually, I'm guessing. As I say, I know very little about him.

I hope you enjoy this book as much as I did. As you might expect from someone who moved from saving face to saving lives, it is a really original piece of work.

John Lloyd
Oxfordshire, September 2013

A

Agglethorpe • Ainderby Quernhow •

Azerley • Ampleforth •

Allerton Mauleverer •

Arthursdale • Askham Bryan •

Adwalton • Acaster Malbis •

Altofts •

Agbrigg •

Arksey • Adlingfleet •

Abdy • Aukley •

Aston •

Abdy *(n.) SY*

A button on a television remote with no identifiable purpose.

Acaster Malbis *(n.) NY*

The only character to appear in both *Star Wars* and *Harry Potter.*

Adlingfleet *(n.) EY*

A tactically spread out stream of inebriated young men into a nightclub with a 'no stag do' policy.

Adwalton *(n.) WY*

One who describes their holiday in a good deal more detail than was asked for.

Agbrigg *(v.) WY*

To greatly exaggerate details of a personal anecdote before realising that one of the people listening was there at the time.

Agglethorpe *(n.) NY*

Someone who doggedly goes on bargaining when the vendor is clearly not budging on price.

Ainderby Quernhow *(n.) NY*

One who finds sexual innuendo in the most innocent of contexts.

Allerton Mauleverer *(n.) NY*

A newly purchased item of furniture that definitely looks like it should fit through the door but, after half an hour of backbreaking manoeuvring, definitely doesn't.

Altofts *(pl.n.) WY*

The bits missed when shaving, first noticed on getting home at night from an important meeting or a first date.

Ampleforth *(v.) NY*

To stride confidently onto the dance floor at the office Christmas party, having spent the first half of the evening drinking oneself into the necessary state of self-assurance.

Arksey *(v.) SY*

The tilt of an imaginary pint glass to ask if someone on the other side of a noisy pub wants a drink.

Arthursdale *(n.) WY*

The slowest drinker in a round.

Askham Bryan *(n.) NY*

A child who replies to every answer with the question "but why?".

Aston *(n.) SY*

A perfect retort composed an hour and a half too late.

Aukley *(adj.) SY*

Having an irrational and pointless personal hatred for any form of malfunctioning technology – computers, DVD players, mobile phones, sat nav, etc.

Azerley *(adj.) NY*

Fuzzy and disoriented after 3pm on Christmas day.

B

Boosbeck
Borrowby

Beckermonds   Bagby ● Balk

● Brackenbottom   Burton Fleming   Bempton

Bordley   Boynton
Blubberhouses   Burnt Yates
Beamsley
Ben Rhydding   Burley in Wharfedale
Bramhope

Boulderclough   ● Bailiff Bridge   Bubwith   Burstwick

Badsworth
Brodsworth   ● Barnby Dun
Brampton Bierlow   ● Blaxton
Bentley Rise
Birley Carr ● Bradgate

Badsworth *(n.) WY*

One who consistently gets frisked at airport security.

Bagby *(n.) NY*

The phantom shoulder bag that causes a brief moment of panic before realising you didn't come out with it in the first place.

Baliff Bridge *(n.) WY*

The point halfway through an amusing anecdote where you hand over to a better storyteller who was also involved.

Balk *(n.) NY*

The thing you stubbornly refuse to put down despite the fact it's making what you're trying to do twice as difficult.

Barnby Dun *(n.) SY*

The mystery person who manages to leave a public toilet in an inexplicably unpleasant state.

Beamsley *(n.)* NY

The superior smirk only found on the faces of BBC royal correspondents.

Beckermonds *(pl.n.)* NY

People in a relationship who clearly shouldn't be.

Bempton *(n.)* EY

A complete stranger who inexplicably singles you out for a buffeting on the dodgems.

Bempton

Ben Rhydding *(ptcpl.v.)* WY

Communicating entirely in football banter.

Bentley Rise *(n.)* SY

The action of sitting down in the dining room of a B&B then getting straight up again on realising it's buffet service.

Birley Carr *(n.)* SY

A badly parked vehicle taking up two spaces in a packed car park.

Birley Carr

Blaxton *(n.) SY*

An inappropriate text or email sent to the wrong person.

Blubberhouses *(pl.n.) NY*

Holding areas used for guests on The Jeremy Kyle Show.

Boosbeck *(n.) NY*

The precise, queasy moment you realise you've had too much to drink.

Boulderclough *(v.) WY*

To stumble with much arm flailing down the last few stairs before improbably landing on two feet with a thud.

Bordley *(adj.) NY*

Descriptive of the glazed remembrance, about three-quarters of the way through the game, that you've never really liked Monopoly that much.

Borrowby *(n.) NY*

The neighbour who's always got the tool you need that isn't worth buying for a one-off DIY job.

Boynton *(n.) EY*

One who irritatingly finger-drums on tabletops, dashboards or any available surface.

Brackenbottom *(n.) NY*

A condition observed in long-haired dogs after they nonchalantly return to their frantic owners following unauthorised adventures in the bushes.

Bradgate *(n.) SY*

A door that, no matter how many times you use it, you always seem to push or pull in the wrong direction.

Bramhope *(n.) WY*

A surprisingly mild hangover.

Brampton Bierlow *(n.)* SY

The chuntering noises made by an old photocopier to let you know that it's thinking about doing something.

Brodsworth *(n.)* SY

An author whose only published book is "An Author's Guide to Publishing".

Bubwith *(n.)* EY

Barely audible stirrings by a baby in the middle of the night that strike fear and despondency into the hearts of its sleep-deprived parents.

Burley in Wharfedale *(n.)* WY

An exotic adventure holiday masquerading as a charity fundraising event, in which the public-spirited participants seek sponsorship to cover the costs of a once-in-a-lifetime experience, generously donating the 2% left over to a worthy cause.

Burnt Yates *(pl.n.)* NY

Toast crumbs found in half-used tubs of butter.

Burstwick *(n.) EY (or Spurn Head (n.) EY)*

A willitoft with something coming out the end of it.

Burton Fleming *(n.) EY*

A pellet of saliva accidentally released during an animated conversation that hits the face of the person you're talking to.

C

Constable Burton
Cowling
Copt Hewick
Crayke
Croome
Claxton
Coniston Cold
Cherry Burton
Crossflats
Cackleshaw
Cullingworth
Cragg Vale
Crigglestone
Campsall
Cudworth
Clayton
Cubley
Cusworth
Cundy Cross
Canklow

Cackleshaw *(v.)* WY

To half-laugh with someone whilst half-laughing at them.

Campsall *(n.)* SY

The alarm experienced by a determinedly heterosexual male who finds himself standing in an inexplicably effeminate posture.

Canklow *(v.)* SY

To punch or kick an inanimate object or surface after hurting oneself on it.

Cherry Burton *(n.)* EY

The rosy pallor of a butcher's face.

Claxton *(n.)* NY

A spurt of uncharacteristically fast-paced typing enjoyed by someone who's usually a very slow typist.

Clayton *(n.)* SY

A small trowel-like implement used by cabin crew to apply foundation.

Coniston Cold *(n.) NY*

An authentic-sounding illness invented to convince one's boss when phoning in sick, the morning after an unscheduled midweek night out. The symptoms of a coniston cold are usually delivered in an ilkley (q.v.) voice.

Constable Burton *(n.) NY*

One who whistles too loudly, too early in the morning.

Copt Hewick *(n.) NY*

An amusing or inappropriate word produced by predictive text.

Cowling *(ptcpl.v.) NY*

Rebelliously walking against the arrows when shopping in Ikea.

Cragg Vale *(n.) WY*

A scar left by a crigglestone.

Crayke *(v.) NY*

To tap the top of a beer can to stop it frothing up when cracking it open. No one knows if this makes any difference.

Crigglestone *(n.) WY*

The tiny piece of grit in the tread of your shoe designed to scratch other people's new wooden floors.

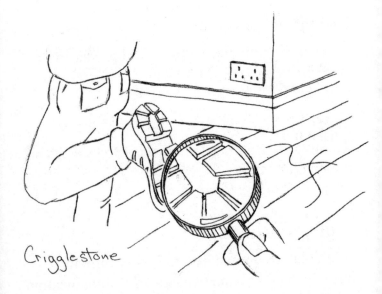

Crigglestone

Croome *(v.)* EY

To lock eyes with someone inside a parked car in the process of checking out one's appearance in their window.

Crossflatts *(n.)* WY

The resentful glares of the occupants of a crowded lift or train forced into close proximity of someone with a particularly unpleasant and contagious cold.

Cubley *(n.)* SY

A burly, intimidating-looking man trying his best to appear meek in the presence of old ladies, small children or vicars.

Cudworth *(n.)* SY

A sound bite from a football manager's post-match press conference.

Cullingworth *(n.)* WY

A foreplay technique that does very little for one's partner yet, due to a lack of communication and imagination, invariably gets thrown into the mix.

Cundy Cross *(adj.) SY*

Artificially angry following a row, long after an apology has been offered, as in "You're just being cundy cross now!"

Cusworth *(n.) SY*

A twee alternative to swearing after stubbing one's toe in the company of children.

D

Darton

Dalby-cum Skewsby

Dropping-Well

Dringhoe

Dunswell

Drax

Drub

Drewton

Durkar

Denby Vale

Denby Main

Dunford Bridge

Dungworth

Dalby-cum-Skewsby *(n.) NY*

The angelic reaching out of an infant's soft hand towards a parent's face before devilishly gouging a facial orifice with all the strength its tiny fingers can muster.

Darton *(n.) SY*

A repeated miss when attempting to put a pen into one's breast pocket.

Denaby Main *(n.) SY*

The item on a restaurant menu chosen by one of a group of diners and envied by all the others, who considered ordering it but went for a less impressive alternative. 'Dave felt a surge of satisfaction as he tucked in to his Denaby Main, exultantly aware of the embittered scowls of his companions'.

Denby Dale

Denby Dale *(n.)* WY

Someone who finds it genuinely amusing to make "bunny ears" behind people's heads in photographs.

Drax *(n.)* NY

A nickname that never really stuck.

Drewton *(n.)* EY

The child in the school photograph with its eyes closed.

Dringhoe *(n.) EY*

One whose idea of popular entertainment is to run through their novelty ring-tone options in public.

Dropping-well *(ptcpl.v.) SY*

The next stage of recovery after passing midhopestones.

Drub *(adj.) WY*

Exhausted by watching too much daytime television.

Dunford Bridge *(n.) SY*

A disastrous topic of conversation embarked upon between two recently acquainted party guests that's even worse than the awkward silence which preceded it.

Dungworth *(n.) SY*

One who conveniently has to go to the toilet whenever there's work to be done.

Dunswell *(n.) EY*

A child's feigned expression of interest in the front of a birthday card, before opening it up to see how much cash falls out.

Durkar *(n.) WY*

A circuitous route designed to avoid charity muggers and Big Issue sellers.

Durkar

E

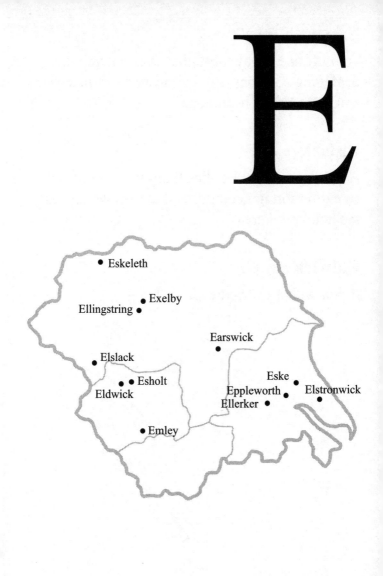

- Eskeleth
- Exelby
- Ellingstring
- Earswick
- Elslack
- Esholt
- Eldwick
- Eske
- Eppleworth
- Elstronwick
- Ellerker
- Emley

Earswick *(v.) NY*

To bluff one's way through a conversation in a deafening environment, by means of shrugs, grins and enthusiastic head nods.

Elslack *(n.) NY*

A holidaymaker who flies thousands of miles to an exotic foreign country and then never leaves the hotel pool area.

Eldwick *(n.) WY*

A pen with a chewed end.

Ellerker *(n.) EY*

A supermarket trip spent repeatedly bumping into the same person you hardly know, having used up all available pleasantries in the fruit and veg aisle.

Ellingstring *(n.) NY*

An unusually long and randomly-located body hair.

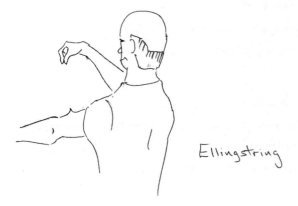

Ellingstring

Elstronwick *(n.) EY*

A bizarre valediction used by the last person to sign an office leaving-card after all the obvious "best wishes", "good luck" and "nice working with you" messages have been claimed.

Emley *(adj.)* WY

Blissfully and eerily silent in the aftermath of a riotous children's birthday party.

Eppleworth *(n.)* EY

One who places Internet access somewhere between food and oxygen in their hierarchy of needs.

Esholt *(n.)* WY

A stock answer to a tediously predictable question about one's occupation.

Eske *(n.)* EY

The mild tingle of excitement experienced when getting into a favourite winter coat on the first nippy day of autumn.

Eskeleth *(n.)* NY

The phase of the moon that brings all the worst drivers out at the same time.

Exelby *(n)* NY

The world-changing idea that strikes in the middle of the night but doesn't seem quite so good in the morning.

F

Faceby •

Fylingdales •

• Fearby

• Foxup

Flamborough •
Fimber

Follifoot • • Full Sutton
•
Fridaythorpe

Fulneck Moravian Settlement

Flinton •
Fitling •

Flockton • • Foulby
•
Farnley Tyas

Faceby *(n.) NY*

A status update announcing to the waiting world that someone is about to do the washing up, go for a nap, pop to the shops etc.

Farnley Tyas *(n.) WY*

A role undertaken by an actor transparently seeking an Oscar nomination, such as one involving learning difficulties, homosexuality or being a member of the Royal family.

Fearby *(n.) NY*

The realisation, far too late, that a hairdresser has wildly misinterpreted or completely ignored your instructions.

Fimber *(v.) EY*

Of amorous teenage boys, to ham-fistedly explore the clasp of a girlfriend's bra, prior to the daunting task of actually getting it undone.

Fitling *(n.) EY*

An uneasy feeling that something of crucial significance has not been packed, when well on the way to the airport or ferry terminal.

Flamborough *(n.) EY*

A leap back in embarrassment after a cooing approach to a mother and baby, on finding a breast-feeding session in full swing.

Flaxby *(n.) NY*

Someone who is congenitally incapable of throwing a Frisbee.

Flinton *(n.) EY*

Darting movement of the head when unsure of greeting etiquette: which side to kiss; one kiss or two; whether to kiss, hug, handshake or hi-five; whether to kiss at all…

Flockton *(n.) WY*

A group of pedestrians at a pelican crossing who will be there till Doomsday because none of them has thought to press the button.

Follifoot *(n.) NY*

An extra, unexpected step encountered when going down a flight of stairs in the dark. Follifeet can result in a minor boulderclough (see also luddenden foot).

Foulby *(n.)* *WY*

Someone who hasn't cleaned their teeth for a year and enjoys standing very close to people when talking to them (see also nostel).

Foxup *(n.)* *NY*

The sudden realisation that you're being flirted with.

Fridaythorpe *(n.)* *EY*

A gaggle of after-work drinkers in Wetherspoons, bent on blotting out the memory of another working week.

Fylingdales

Fylingdales *(pl.n.)* *NY*

An adolescent male's first attempt at sideburns.

Full Sutton *(n.)* *EY*

A satisfyingly successful nose blow (see also kirkby overblow).

Fulneck Moravian Settlement *(n.)* *WY*

The facial contortion adopted to avoid getting toothpaste froth all over your pyjamas, used when trying to talk and brush one's teeth at the same time.

G

- Glaisdale •
- Gammersgill
- Galphay •
- Grimstone •
- Giggleswick
- Great Ouseburn •
- Gembling •
- Glusburn
- Guiseley
- Goodmanham •
- Gomersal •
- Gawber
- Grimethorpe •
- Grenoside •
- Greasbrough
- Gleadless •
- Gildingwells

Galphay *(n.) NY*

The awareness and clarity gained from lying on a quiet beach when the temperature is just right.

Gawber *(v.) SY*

To gaze intently at the ceiling, at the floor, at your phone – anywhere but the direction of the attractive stranger opposite, when under the baleful eye of your other half.

Gammersgill *(v.) NY*

To put on an item of clothing inside-out or the wrong way round, correct it, and then realise it was the right way on to begin with.

Gembling *(ptcpl.v.) EY*

Subtly yet competitively positioning oneself on a railway platform as a train pulls into the station, so as to be adjacent to a door when it stops.

Giggleswick *(n.) NY*

An almost uncontrollable urge to burst out laughing during a funeral.

Gildingwells *(pl.n.) SY*

People with nothing whatsoever in common, forced to spend a great deal of time together because their partners are best friends.

Glaisdale *(v.) NY*

To peruse a menu for several minutes without reading a single word.

Gleadless *(adj.) SY*

Pleasantly devoid of thought.

Glusburn *(v.) NY*

To spray hot wax everywhere when over-enthusiastically blowing out a candle.

Gomersal *(n.) EY*

A botched attempt to say goodbye to someone in the street before awkwardly heading off in the same direction.

Goodmanham *(n.)* EY

The generous and easygoing driver in front of you at a junction who gives way to every single vehicle, unaware that, with every appreciative wave and nod they receive, you are running increasingly late.

Greasbrough *(n.)* SY

The telltale footprint after mopping a kitchen floor in your socks.

Great Ouseburn *(n.)* NY

A mutated grimston.

Grenoside *(n.)* SY

A forgotten moment of drunken stupidity suddenly recalled. "It wasn't until he spotted the empty jam jar and monkey outfit at the end of the bed that Rupert remembered his appalling act of grenoside".

Grimethorpe *(n.)* SY

The tide-line of dirt, dead skin, soap scum and loose hair in a bath after a long soak.

Grimston *(n.) EY*

An ugly-looking spot that would have vanished in a day if only it had been left alone.

Guiseley *(n.) WY*

A trick children use to avoid doing any work in the classroom by starting a teacher off on his or her favourite topic of conversation.

H

Hutton Rudby ●
Hinderwell ●
Honlsyke
● Hauxwell
Hardraw ●
● Hutton Hang
Hummanby ●
Haisthorpe
Hessay ● Haxby ●
● Holtby
● Hanlith
High Gardham
Heptonstall
High Hunsley ● Humbleton ●
● Hebden Royd
Halsham ●
Hipperholme ● ● Hanging Heaton
Haigh ● ● Hampole
● Hexthorpe
● Hoylandswaine
Hooton Levitt ● Hellaby
Hackenthorpe ●

Hackenthorpe *(n.) SY*

The clutch of smokers huddling outside a public building in winter.

Haigh *(v.) SY*

To drunkenly shush an inanimate object when blundering home after a late night.

Haisthorpe *(n.) EY*

The brief pause as one ponders which way to place the toilet roll on the holder.

Halsham *(n.) EY*

A shifty use of a neighbour's wheelie bin because yours is full.

Hampole *(n.) SY*

A fencepost used to display a child's dropped glove.

Hampole

Hanging Heaton *(n.)* *WY*

A pocket of flatulence trapped in a soft chair beneath its perpetrator.

Hanlith *(n.)* *NY*

A note scribbled on one's hand when short of a piece of paper.

Hardraw *(n.)* *NY*

A drawer used for random things that don't fit into any particular category.

Hauxwell *(v.)* *NY*

To add unnecessary ingredients to a dish, simply because they are available or need to be used up, giving the chef a tremendous sense of experimental panache.

Haxby *(n.)* *NY*

Something bought to distract the cashier's attention from the embarrassing item you actually came in for.

Hebden Royd *(v.)* *WY*

The act of spinning flat batteries in the back of the remote in order to magically bring them back to life.

Hellaby *(n.)* *SY*

The ear-splitting noise of bottles dropped into a bottle bank.

Heptonstall *(v.)* *WY*

To sense, shortly after beginning a long story, that no one is really that interested.

Hessay *(v.)* *NY*

To lose the will to live halfway through reading a museum information board.

Hexthorpe *(n.)* *SY*

The magical ability to throw a pair of dice without them rolling off the playing surface and under a piece of furniture.

High Gardham *(n.)* *EY*

That part of a supermarket ceiling examined by a cashier as you enter your pin number.

High Hunsley *(n.) EYx*

The voice you can't help using when confronted by a bully.

Hinderwell *(n.) NY*

A toilet seat that won't stay upright without assistance: male users are obliged to awkwardly keep it up with one knee, but female users are surprised and delighted that someone has apparently left it down for their use.

Hipperholme *(n.) WY*

A five-mile tailback caused by parents driving their newborn baby home from the hospital for the first time.

Holtby *(n.) NY*

The point at which a four-legged chair is at its two-legged tilt limit.

Hooton Levitt *(n.) SY*

The quick-witted person at a party who spontaneously delivers the same side-splitting one-liner you had just spent the past hour ingeniously concocting.

Houlsyke *(n.) NY*

The high-pitched screaming noise emitted by fairground ghost trains.

Hoylandswaine *(n.) SY*

The subtle onscreen chemistry between two TV presenters that hints at a deep-rooted hatred simmering behind their gleaming smiles.

Humbleton *(n.) NY*

Someone whose harsh life experience provides you with a feeling of much needed perspective.

Hunmanby *(n.) NY*

The silent empathy of downtrodden men waiting outside ladies' changing rooms.

Hutton Hang *(n.) NY*

An offered handshake that is pointedly ignored or goes completely unnoticed.

Hutton Rudby *(n.) NY*

A man with an improbably large penis who spends an unnecessary amount of time strutting around the changing room pretending to dry himself.

I

Ivelet

Irton

Ilkley

Illingworth

Ilkley *(adj)* WY

Descriptive of the voice used when phoning in sick with a coniston cold (q.v.).

Illingworth *(n.)* WY

Someone who spends way too much time on the Internet.

Irton *(n.)* NY

The faint suspicion that one's entrance into a room has coincided with a sudden change in the topic of conversation.

Ivelet *(n.)* NY

The white safety line round an airport baggage carousel put there so everyone has something to ignore.

J

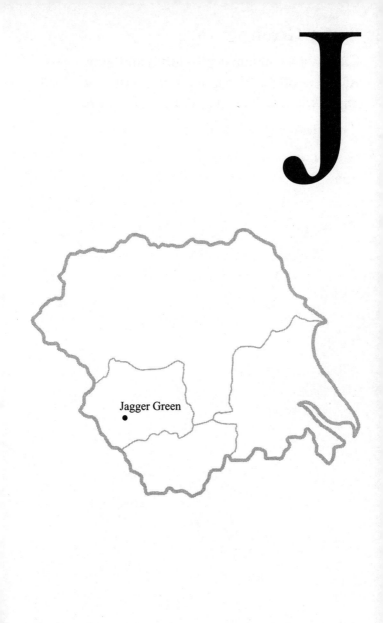

Jagger Green

Jagger Green *(adj.) SY*

The envy of the musically gifted but ugly members of a rock band for the charismatic lead singer who can't even play the tambourine.

K

Kettlewell

Kirkby Malzeard

Knipe Point

Kirkby Overblow

Kilnwick Percy

Kiplingcotes

Knedlington

Kilpin

Kirkheaton

Kettlewell *(n.) NY*

Someone whose solution to all of life's adverse circumstances is to make a cup of tea.

Kilnwick Percy *(n.) EY*

One who ruins a film by continually whispering that the book was better.

Kilpin *(n.) EY*

The first child in a school year to suggest that Father Christmas doesn't exist.

Kiplingcotes *(pl.n.) NY*

Jackets with too many pockets that result in a lifetime of wasted minutes fumbling for bank cards, keys, phones and train tickets.

Kirkby Malzeard *(n.) NY*

Someone who recounts their dreams in minute detail as if they were real life events.

Kirkby Overblow *(n.) NY*

A full sutton that causes one's ears to burst.

Kirkheaton *(n.) WY*

Suppressed rage resulting from being unable to enter into a full-blown marital row due to the presence of one's in-laws .

Knedlington *(n.) EY*

The softly spoken inner voice of reason, heard but ignored, shortly before committing an act of grenoside.

Knipe Point *(n.) NY*

The point in a bad novel when the reader first suspects they're not going to finish it.

L

Lazenby

Loftus

Leeming

Long Preston
Linton

Little Ouseburn
Leavening

Little Kelk

Lund

Lelly

Luddendenfoot
Linthwaite

Laughton en
le Morthern
Letwell

Lazenby *(n.) NY*

One whose laid-back charm successfully disguises a bone idle slothfulness.

Laughton en le Morthen *(n.) SY*

The pregnant pause after a child falls over that, depending on the reaction of any adult watching, will end in either a merry gurgle or half an hour of blood-curdling screams.

Leavening *(ptpcl.v.) NY*

Working out when to set off to catch a flight.

Leeming *(ptpcl.v.) NY*

Squeezing the trigger on a petrol pump in little bursts, in an attempt to hit a round number on the dial.

Lelley *(n.) EY*

A waft of the duvet after breaking wind in bed.

Letwell *(v.) SY*

To stoically continue looking interested during an exchange of views, whilst battling to hold onto a relevant thought to be imparted when the conversation finally allows.

Lelley

Linthwaite *(n.) WY*

A small piece of fluff on a carpet that seems immune to the sucking of a vacuum cleaner.

Linton *(n.) WY*

A suit that requires a last-minute sponge and press, due to the fact that it is only ever worn at weddings, ends up in a crumpled mess by the bed, and then gets hurriedly stashed away until the cycle begins again on the morning of the next wedding.

Little Kelk *(n.)* EY

The child most likely to make a supply teacher's day a living hell.

Little Ouseburn *(n.)* NY

A rogue piece of scalding hot pizza topping that burns your chin.

Loftus *(n.)* NY

A regional gift title book transparently replicating and riding on the tailcoats of an already established and successful bestseller.

Long Preston *(n.)* NY

Someone who stubbornly refuses to make a phone call when a time-consuming series of long-winded text messages can be exchanged instead.

Luddendenfoot *(n.)* WY

A landing at the bottom of a darkened staircase that arrives one step earlier than expected (see also follifoot).

Lund *(v.)* EY

To clumsily stumble onto a luddendenfoot.

M

- Muker
- Malton End
- Muston
- Midgley
- Methley
- Mixenden
- Meaux
- Metham
- Micklebring
- Midhopestones
- Morthen

Meaux *(adj.)* EY

Descriptive of the squeamish feeling brought on by looking at a bath in a cheap hotel, knowing that hundreds of bottoms of all shapes and sizes have previously been there.

Metham *(n.)* EY

The thin wire mesh around a bottle of wine to show it's a bit more expensive.

Methley *(n.)* WY

A perfunctory brushing of the teeth before sex.

Micklebring *(n.)* SY

Randomly selected reading material hastily picked up on the way to the toilet.

Midgley *(n.)* WY

A school bully's smaller, ratty-looking sidekick.

Midhopestones *(pl.n.)* SY

The first relatively solid stools passed after a bad case of diarrhoea, signalling that the worst may be over (see also dropping well).

Mixenden *(n.)* WY

The amusing accent acquired by a foreign professional footballer living in England.

Morthen *(n.)* SY

An exaggerated Northern accent used when dealing with salt-of-the-earth Yorkshire tradesmen in the hope it will give the impression you know more about what you're paying for than you actually do.

Moulton End *(n.)* NY

The stage in a relationship when using the toilet in front of each other is no longer an issue.

Muker *(v.)* NY

To retch slightly when using a toothbrush to clean the back of one's tongue.

Muston *(adj.)* NY

Descriptive of the allegedly authentic Viking smell on the ride at the Yorvik Viking Centre in York.

N

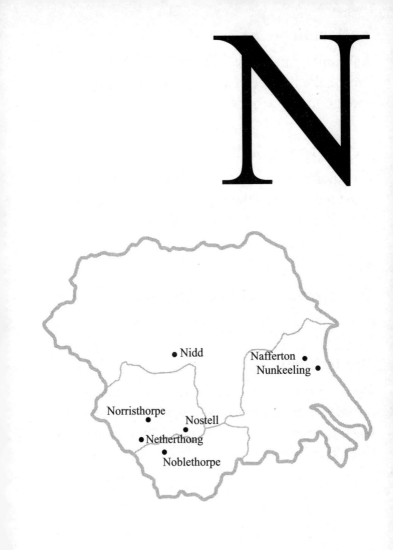

Nidd

Nafferton
Nunkeeling

Norristhorpe

Nostell

Netherthong

Noblethorpe

Nafferton *(n.)* EY

A fumbling attempt at a complex 'urban' handshake between two friends who are old enough to know better.

Netherthong *(n.)* WY

A withered item of underwear only ever worn as a last resort when the laundry basket is full and absolutely no other options exist.

Nidd *(n.)* NY

The chopped and discarded end of a root vegetable.

Noblethorpe *(n.)* SY

One approached by a bartender who indicates it's not their turn to be served and kindly points out the flustered person who's gone unnoticed for the last ten minutes.

Norristhorpe

Norristhorpe *(n.)* *WY*

The first person in a motorway traffic jam to get out of their car and walk about sighing.

Nostell *(v.)* *WY*

To alter the timing of one's breathing to avoid inhaling the rancid breath of a foulby.

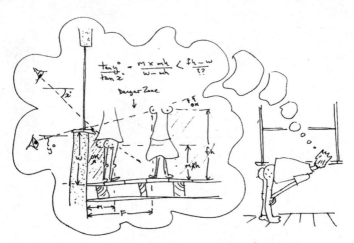

Nunkeeling

Nunkeeling *(ptcpl.v.) EY*

Bending to determine the eye-line between one's
body parts and the windowsill, to see what might
have been on view to the neighbours after getting
changed with the curtains open.

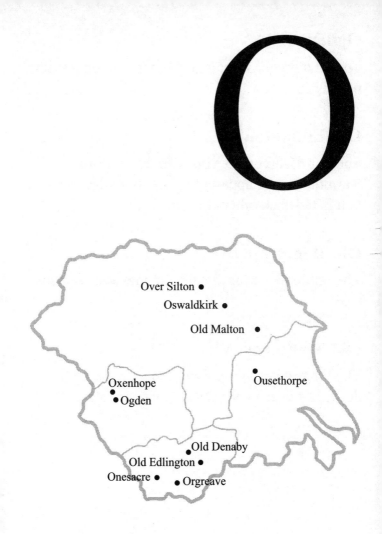

Over Silton ●

Oswaldkirk ●

Old Malton ●

● Ousethorpe

Oxenhope
● Ogden

Old Denaby
Old Edlington ●
Onesacre ● ● Orgreave

Ogden *(v.)* WY

To feel a pregnant woman's bump without asking permission.

Old Edlington *(n.)* SY

Someone who greets you with discomforting warmth, having apparently forgotten how much you hated each other at school.

Old Denaby *(n.)* SY

The polite name for the unsold crap at a car boot sale.

Old Malton *(n.)* NY

The longest surviving food item in a freezer, destined never to be thrown away or eaten.

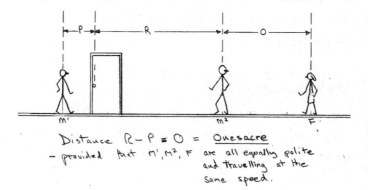

Distance $R - P = O = \underline{\text{Onesacre}}$
- provided that m^1, m^2, F are all equally polite and travelling at the same speed.

Onesacre *(n.) SY*

The distance between two people approaching the same door, creating a dilemma for the first person to get there: holding it open obligates the second person to quicken their pace out of politeness, whereas not holding it open might be considered rude...

Orgreave *(v.) SY*

To lament having just bought something on discovering another one elsewhere for half the price.

Oswaldkirk *(n.)* *NY*

A backpacker who picks up an affected Australian accent from three months down-under and then manages to hold onto it for six months after returning home.

Ousethorpe *(n.)* *EY*

The moisture remaining on the hands after being subjected to the feeble breaths of the average pub hand-dryer, traditionally removed on items of clothing.

Over Silton *(n.)* *NY*

The stage of a fancy dress party when the novelty of everyone's costumes has worn off and everything just feels a bit weird.

Oxenhope *(v.)* *WY*

To gamely insert into a conversation a recently acquired impressive-sounding word whose meaning, or context in which it should be used, you are not quite sure of.

P

Pinchinthorpe

Pockley

Potter Brompton

Plompton

Piccadilly

Pontefract

Patrington Haven

Plumbley

Patrington Haven *(n.)* EY

Someone who feigns reluctance to perform their celebrated party piece whilst milking the adoring pleas of the other guests.

Piccadilly *(v.)* SY

To dance up and down a line of unsanitary toilet cubicles, trying to decide which one to use.

Pinchinthorpe *(n.) NY*

Someone who returns for another free sample of whatever is being given away at the supermarket.

Plompton *(n.) NY*

One who has expanded beyond plumbley.

Plumbley *(adj.) SY*

Attractively slightly overweight, e.g. "Elaine was a plumbley lass".

Pockley *(adj) NY*

Descriptive of the look achieved by applying too much concealer on spotty skin.

Pontefract *(n.) WY*

The strange look you get from revealing a recently acquired secret to the person who swore you to secrecy in the first place.

Potter Brompton *(n.) NY*

A small DIY task of such insignificance that it never gets done.

Queensbury

Queensbury *(n.) WY*

The immaculately turned out lady at the gym who seems to have no sweat glands.

R

Ruswarp •

Rievaulx •

• Rathmell

Ruston Parva •

Rotsea •

• Rolston

• Ryther cum Ossendyke

Routh

Roos •

• Riddlesden

• Ripponden

• Reedness

• Royd

Rathmell *(n.) NY*

The increasing tightness in one's chest when placed on hold for more than two hours.

Reedness *(n.) EY*

Mingled anxiety and curiosity on seeing an unrecognised number come up on your mobile phone.

Riddlesden *(n.) WY*

A roll of sticky tape with no apparent starting point.

Rievaulx *(n.) NY*

The rare gift of being able to outstare an expressionless old Frenchman.

Ripponden *(n.) WY*

The sequence of panic, relief, judgement and righteous indignation on hearing a mobile phone interrupt a play or a wedding and realising it's someone else's.

Rolston *(n.) EY*

A shopping trolley with a wonky wheel.

Roos *(pl.n.) EY*

Wayne Rooney-related tabloid headlines, such as "WOULD ROO BELIEVE IT!", "WE'RE TH-ROO", "I ONLY HAVE EYES FOR ROO", "ROO-MARKABLE", etc.

Routh *(n.) EY*

Adrenaline-fuelled rage and despair at 11.45pm on a Sunday night caused by the music reverberating through the bedroom wall from the students next door.

Rotsea *(n.) EY*

The blessed release of suppressed wind after parting company from a new lover the morning after a first night together.

Royd *(n.) SY*

A unit of adrenaline released by a driver aquaplaning at speed on a flooded motorway.

Ruswarp *(v.) NY*

To deliberately write a word unclearly when you don't know how to spell it.

Ruston Parva *(n.) EY*

Awareness of the direction of one's gaze when sitting close to a breastfeeding mother: 'Bob entered a state of ruston parva after his earlier flamborough'.

Ryther cum Ossendyke *(n.) NY*

The cloud of awkwardness that descends on a family living room during an unexpected TV sex scene.

S

- Skeeby
- Sinnington
- Silpho
- Scalby
- Stalling Busk
- Spaunton
- Sharrow
- Scampston
- Speeton
- Studley Roger
- Scagglethorpe
- Swinden
- Scriven
- Staveley
- Skerne
- Sicklinghall
- Skirpenbeck
- Skipwith
- Skirlaugh
- Sancton
- Sproatley
- Shibden
- Sandholme
- Skidby
- Scammonden
- Swinefleet
- Skeffling
- Slaithwaite
- Scissett
- Sharlston
- Skelmanthorpe
- Shafton
- Skellow

Sancton *(n.) EY*

The minimum distance from a city where it becomes socially acceptable to smile and nod at strangers.

Sandholme *(n.) EY*

The spot finally selected on a crowded beach after trudging about with three bags, a picnic box and a windbreak for twenty minutes, rejecting almost identical areas.

Scagglethorpe *(n.) NY*

The collective noun for red-faced January joggers who are nowhere to be seen by early February.

Scalby *(n.) EY*

A shower that swings from scalding hot or icy cold without ever settling in between.

Scammonden *(n.) WY*

Someone who calls a mobile phone and lets it ring once, so the other person will call back and save them using up their credit.

Scampston *(n.) NY*

A queue-jumper who is apparently unaware how much everyone else loathes them.

Scissett *(n.) WY*

A secret told in strictest confidence that both parties know will be impossible to keep.

Scriven *(n.) NY*

Dried toothpaste around the nozzle of the tube.

Shafton *(n.) SY*

One who blithely overtakes a long line of obediently queuing drivers and then successfully cuts into the required lane at the last moment.

Sharlston *(n.) WY*

A person who describes their taste in music as "eclectic" whose CD collection consists of three 80s movie soundtracks, Abba's Greatest Hits and a Dido album.

Sharrow *(n.) SY*

The lingering agony after banging one's shin that goes on and on and on.

Shibden *(v.)* WY

To sift through a Sunday newspaper, filtering out the numerous sections of no interest.

Sicklinghall *(n.)* NY

A wrecked living room full of snoring people no one knows, the morning after a teenager's party in the parents' absence.

Silpho *(n.)* NY

A man who stands unnecessarily close to others at a urinal.

Silpho

Sinnington *(n.) NY*

Someone who thinks it's original to stick chewing gum under furniture.

Skeeby *(n.) NY*

One who leaves a tip and then hangs around to see what kind of reaction it gets.

Skeffling *(ptcpl.v.) EY*

What drunken students are doing with stolen traffic cones.

Skeffling

Skellow *(v.)* SY

Of a dinner party host to consciously wind down conversation at the end of the evening to let guests know they really should be leaving soon.

Skelmanthorpe *(n.)* WY

Hoarded instruction manuals for electrical equipment that has long since gone.

Skerne *(v.)* EY

To accidentally toenail-gouge one's partner in bed.

Skidby *(n.)* EY

Something left behind by a barnby dunn.

Skipwith *(n.)* NY

The most inappropriate guilty pleasure an mp3 player could select when in shuffle mode at a sophisticated dinner party.

Skirlaugh *(n.)* EY

The insufferably loud cackle of a particular type of alpha-female.

Skirpenbeck *(v.) EY*

To enter a deserted gift shop, say hello to the hopeful owner, quickly realise there is nothing of interest for sale, and then immediately leave.

Slaithwaite *(v.) WY*

To keep one eye shut when having a pee in the middle of the night.

Spaunton *(n.) NY*

A freakishly lucky pot in snooker or pool (see also swinden).

Speeton *(n.) NY*

Blatantly obvious information provided by a young estate agent showing clients round a property.

Sproatley *(adj.) EY*

Descriptive of the general demeanour of someone who never really stood much of a chance in life.

Stalling Busk *(ptcpl.v.) NY*

Late-night channel flicking that keeps you up way beyond your bedtime.

Staveley *(adj.) NY*

Alarmed by catching a rarely observed reflection of oneself in profile in a multi-mirrored washroom.

Studley Roger *(n.) NY*

A partner's panic-inducing ex-boyfriend who seems to possess every single quality a girl could wish for in a man.

Swinden *(n.) NY*

One who chalks their cue with cool indifference to give the impression that the spaunton (q.v.) was fully intended.

Swinefleet *(v.) EY*

To select from the lower tray in a box of chocolates, despite the fact there are still a few nasty-looking jobs to be eaten on the top one.

T

- Thwaite
- Thornton Watlass
- Thwing
- Tosside
- Timble
- Tockwith
- Tickton
- Thirtleby
- Thorngumbald
- Tankersley
- Todwick

Tankersley *(adj.)* SY

Descriptive of the look on the faces of fat people eating junk food who know they are being judged.

Thirtleby *(n.)* EY

A mature lady suddenly rummaging through her handbag, after queuing placidly at the supermarket checkout for the previous ten minutes.

Thorngumbald *(n.)* NY

An elderly gentleman who spends three minutes rubbing his chin and squinting into the distance before confirming that no, he doesn't know the way to wherever it is you urgently need to get to.

Thornton Watlass *(n.)* NY

A man who winks indiscriminately in an attempt to appear suave or charming.

Thwaite *(v.)* NY

To pat one's pockets to let others know you're making an effort to look for something.

Thwing *(v.)* EY

To lip-sync a hymn at a church wedding. This may result from not knowing the tune, fear of singing in public, or an inability to settle on an octave that will suit the chorus.

Tickton *(n.)* EY

A business meeting with the sole purpose of enabling colleagues to run through the minutes of the last meeting before writing up the minutes of this one.

Timble *(v.)* NY

To remove skid marks in a toilet basin by urinating on them: a practical solution to an embarrassing problem, or a game, depending on circumstances.

Todwick *(n.)* SY

One who can be relied upon to back out of a social occasion at the last minute.

Tosside *(n.)* NY

A mysterious ball of used tissue on the bedroom floor.

Tockwith *(n.) NY*

Someone who sets all their clocks and watches a few minutes fast.

U

Ugthorpe (n.) NY

The group of bigger boys at the back of the school bus.

Ulley (v.) SY

To frequently change position around a bonfire to avoid the prevailing direction of smoke.

Ulley

Ulrome (v.) EY

When trying out new shoes, to tour the shop in a stiff and self-conscious manner.

Upper Poppleton (n.) NY

The blobs of congealed food on the inner roof of a student's microwave.

V

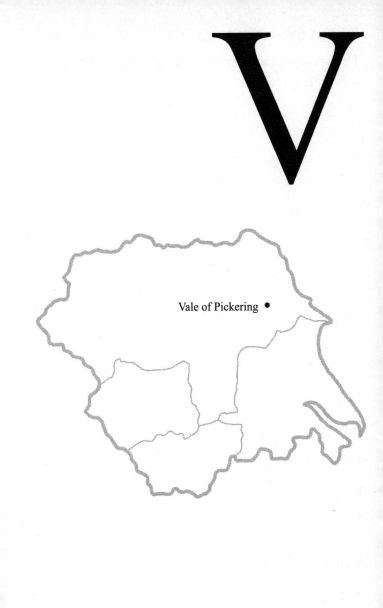

Vale of Pickering ●

Vale of Pickering *(n.)*

The alley behind the bike sheds where school bullies lie in wait.

W

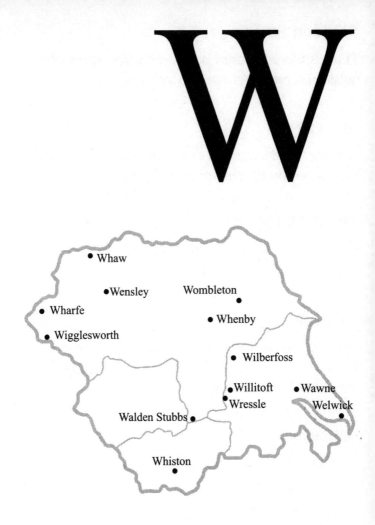

Walden Stubbs *(n.) NY*

Names in your phone's address book of people who are completely unknown to you.

Wawne *(n.) EY*

The ironic groan from drinkers in a pub or restaurant on hearing smashed glass.

Welwick *(n.) EY*

The sound of a tent zip that induces nostalgia for camping.

Wharfe *(n.) NY*

Loud conversation between successful business men who want you to know you are overhearing successful business men.

Whenby *(n.) NY*

The day after tomorrow.

Wensley *(n.) NY*

The day after whenby.

Whaw *(n.)* *NY*

A loud grunting noise made by any one of the thick-necked men in the gym.

Whiston *(n.)* *SY*

A fleeting, sentimental memory that causes one to smile nostalgically, while self-satisfactorily cocking one's head at the wisdom acquired through such reflection .

Wigglesworth *(n.)* *NY*

A child with an inability to remain still for a single moment.

Wigglesworth

Wilberfoss *(n.) EY*

Lint, fluff and other detritus clinging to lost coins found down the back of a sofa.

Willitoft *(n.) EY*

The classic schoolboy graffiti cock-and-balls image (see also burstwick).

Wombleton *(n.) NY*

The pathetic pretend limp of a professional footballer returning to the pitch after being carried off following five minutes of rolling around, grimacing and arm waving. The wombleton will disappear given sufficient time or a goal scoring opportunity.

Wressle *(n.) EY*

A plastic shopping bag that proves impossible to open, causing a massive build up of purchases at the supermarket checkout.

Y

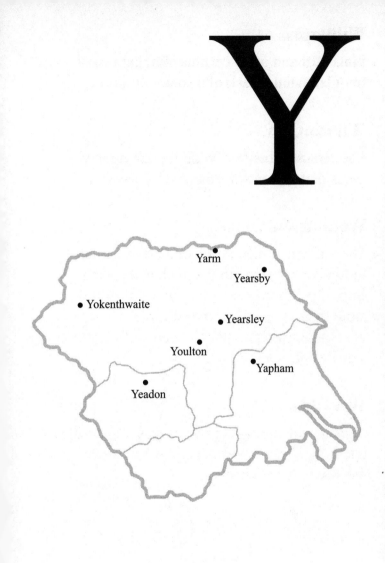

Yarm

Yearsby

Yokenthwaite

Yearsley

Youlton

Yapham

Yeadon

Yapham *(n.) EY*

A nasty aggressive little dog that has only avoided being muzzled because of its size.

Yarm *(n.) NY*

The small amount of liquid remaining in your glass that prompts the bar staff to ask if it's 'dead'.

Yeadon *(n.)* EY

The first household on a street to get a Christmas tree each year, traditionally a week after Bonfire Night.

Yearsley *(n.)* NY

A drunken phone call or text to an ex on New Year's Eve, continued annually until someone better comes along or legal papers are filed.

Yearsby *(n.)* NY

An ex at the receiving end of consecutive yearslys.

Yokenthwaite *(n.)* NY

The egg-smeared residue on a plate after a good fry up, traditionally mopped up with a piece of bread.

Youlton *(n.)* NY

A place name in Yorkshire that sounds like it should be a liff, but isn't yet. Examples include Barton-le-Willows, Berry Brow, Nappa, Duggleby, Sexhow, Scagglethorpe and Bramham cum Oglethorpe, to name but a few…

- THE END -

Acknowledgements
Thank you to the following people:

My wife Emma, because I'd never live it down if I didn't mention her first; my brothers John and Sam for their honest feedback on each and every liff (some now not included in this book), my Dad for his illustrations, created under my critical scrutiny in a matter of weeks to hit the print deadline; my Mum, well 'cos she's my Mum; my sister Anna, because it would be kind of unfair to leave her out; and Bob for randomly texting me about a Radio 4 programme celebrating the anniversary of *The Meaning of Liff*.

John and Sarah Lloyd. I simply can't thank you enough for all you've done.

Oh, and cheers to my mates, who had nothing to do with this book, but you can't say I didn't mention you now.

INDEX OF MEANINGS

BUFFET
standing up for: *Bentley Rise*

BULLIES
Voice when confronting:
High Hunsley
sidekick: *Midgley*
Alley: *Vale of Pickering*

BUSINESSMEN
loud conversation: *Wharfe*

BUTCHERS
pallor of face: *Cherry Burton*

C

CALL CENTRES
being placed on hold: *Rathmell*

CAMPING
nostalgia: *Welwick*

CANDLES
blowing out with gusto:
Glusburn

CARDS
money in: *Dunswell*
leaving card message:
Elstronwick

CAR BOOT SALE
unsold: *Old Denaby*

CARS
badly parked: *Birley Carr*
checking reflection in window:
Croome

fueling-up: *Leeming*
getting out of in queue:
Norristhorpe

CHAIR
tilting: *Holtby*

CHANGING ROOMS
strutting: *Hutton Rudby*

CHARITY COLLECTORS
avoiding: *Durkar*

CHEWING GUM
sticking under: *Sinnington*

CHILDREN
asking questions: *Askham
Bryan*
attempting to appear meek in
presence of: *Cubley*
twee alternative to swearing in
company of: *Cusworth*
with eyes closed in school
photo: *Drewton*
opening cards for money:
Dunswell
trick played on teachers:
Guiseley
falling over: *Laughten en le
Morthen*
hell for teachers: *Little Kelk*
inability to stay still:
Wigglesworth

CHRISTMAS
tired on Christmas Day: *Azerley*
Father Christmas existence:
Kilpin
first to get tree: *Yeadon*

CHOCOLATES

selecting from lower tray:
Swinefleet

CLOCKS

setting fast: *Tockwith*

CLOTHES

winter coat excitement: *Eske*
putting on wrong: *Gammersgill*
too many pockets: *Kiplingcotes*
crumpled suit: *Linton*
last resort underwear:
Netherthong

COOKING

unnecessarily experimental:
Hauxwell

CONVERSATION

recently acquainted party
guests: *Dunford Bridge*
noisy environment: *Earswick*
answer regarding occupation:
Esholt
change of: *Irton*
holding on to thought: *Letwell*
use impressive word: *Oxenhope*
businessmen: *Wharfe*

COUPLES

that shouldn't be together:
Beckermonds
friends of partners:
Gildingwells
suppressed row: *Kirkheaton*

D

DEMEANOR

no chance: *Sproatley*

DICE

ability to throw: *Hexthorpe*

DIRECTIONS

elderly gentleman:
Thorngumbald

DIY

neighbour with tools: *Borrowby*
small task: *Potter Brompton*

DODGEMS

stranger buffeting: *Bempton*

DOGS

condition of fur:
Brackenbottom
little and aggressive: *Yapham*

DOORS

pushing/pulling in wrong
direction: *Bradgate*
holding open: *Onesacre*

DREAMS

recounted: *Kirkby Malzeard*

DRIVING

moons cycle: *Eskeleth*
overly generous: *Goodmanham*
newborn home: *Hipperholme*
aquaplaning: *Royd*
cutting in: *Shafton*

DRUNK

stag do entering nightclub:
Adlingfleet
confidently approaching dance
floor: *Ampleforth*
too much: *Boosbeck*
mild hangover: *Bramhope*
act of stupidity: *Grenoside*
shushing: *Haigh*
ignored voice: *Knedlington*

DRINKING

offering to buy drink: *Arksey*
slowest drinker: *Arthursdale*
after work: *Fridaythorpe*
liquid in glass: *Yarm*

E

EMAILS
sent to the wrong person: *Blaxton*

ESTATE AGENTS
obvious information: *Speeton*

EXAGGERATING
personal anecdote: *Agbrigg*

EXES
partner's: *Studley Roger*
phone call to: *Yearsley*
consecutive yearsleys: *Yearsby*

F

FENCEPOST
used for dropped glove:
Hampole

FILM
Star Wars and Harry Potter:
Acaster Malbis
ruined by: *Kilnwick Percy*

FINGER-DRUMMING
irritatingly: *Boynton*

FLATULENCE
in chair: *Hanging Heaton*
in bed: *Lelly*
morning after: *Rotsea*

FLIGHT
when to leave for: *Leavening*

FLIRTING
realization: *Foxup*
avoiding: *Gawber*

FLUFF
immune to vacuuming:
Linthwaite
side of sofa: *Wilberfoss*

FOOD
crumbs in butter: *Burnt Yates*
best item on menu: *Denaby
Main*
scalding pizza: *Little Ouseburn*
vegetable chopped end: *Nidd*
in freezer: *Old Malton*
fat people eating: *Tankersley*
fry up residue: *Yokenthwaite*

FOOTBALL
banter: *Ben Rhydding*
soundbite from manager:
Cudworth
foreign player's accent:
Mixenden
Rooney headlines: *Roos*
Fake limp: *Wombleton*

FOUNDATION
trowel for cabin crew: *Clayton*
too much: *Pockley*

FRENCHMEN
ability to outstare: *Rievaulx*

FRISBEE
inability to throw: *Flaxby*

FURNITURE
too big to fit through door:
Allerton Mauleverer

G

GAMES
dice: *Hexthorpe*
Monopoly: *Bordley*

GOODBYES
botched: *Gomersal*

GRAFFITI
cock n balls and stuff:
Burstwick
cock n balls: *Willitoft*

GYM
sweat-free lady: *Queensbury*
grunting: *Whaw*

H

HAGGLING
not giving up: *Agglethorpe*

HAIR
body hair: *Ellingstring*
sideburns: *Fylingdales*

HAIRCUT
misinterpretation: *Fearby*

HANDSHAKE
ignored: *Hutton Hang*
failed: *Nafferton*

HOLIDAYS
describing in detail: *Adwalton*
charity adventure holiday:
Burley in Wharfedale
never leaving pool area: *Elslack*

I

IDEAS
world changing: *Exelby*
self reflection: *Whiston*

ILLNESS
invented when phoning in sick:
Coniston Cold
voice Coniston Cold delivered
in: *Ilkley*

resentful glares at people with colds: *Crossflatts*

INSTRUCTION MANUALS
horded: *Skelmanthorpe*

INTERNET
importance: *Eppleworth*
mundane Facebook update: *Faceby*
too much: *Illingworth*

J

JEREMY KYLE SHOW
holding areas: *Blubberhouses*

JOGGERS
January: *Scagglethorpe*

K

KISSING
etiquette: *Flinton*

L

LAUGHING
at and with: *Cackleshaw*
at a funeral: *Giggleswick*
alpha-female: *Skirlaugh*

LIFFS
Youlton

M

MENU
best item on: *Denaby Main*
to stare at: *Glaisdale*

MIRRORS
alarmed by reflection: *Staveley*

MONOPOLY
bored of: *Bordley*

MOPPING
in socks: *Greasbrough*

MUSEUMS
information board: *Hessay*
yorvic smell: *Muston*

MUSIC
lead singer envy: *Jagger Green*
through wall: *Routh*
"eclectic": *Sharlston*

N

NEWSPAPERS
sifting through: *Shibden*

NICKNAMES
temporary: *Drax*

NOSE BLOWING
successful: *Full Sutton*
ears bursting: *Kirkby Overblow*

O

OVERWEIGHT
to suit: *Plumbley*
beyond: *Plompton*
eating: *Tankersley*

P

PAIN
hitting back inanimate object: *Canklow*
banging shin: *Sharrow*

PARTIES
quiet after children's: *Emley*
one-liner: *Hooton Levitt*
fancy dress: *Over Silton*
feigned reluctance: *Patrington Haven*
morning after teenagers': *Sicklinghall*
to wind down: *Skellow*

PEDESTRIAN CROSSING
not pressing button: *Flockton*

PENS
repeated miss in breast pocket: *Darton*
chewed: *Eldwick*

PERSPECTIVE
much needed: *Humbleton*
clear: *Galphay*

PHONES
one who runs through ringtones: *Dringhoe*
only using text: *Long Preston*
placed on hold: *Rathmell*
feeling from unrecognized number: *Reedness*
interrupting: *Ripponden*
ringing once: *Scammonden*
unknown name: *Walden Stubbs*

PHOTOS
one who makes "bunny ears": *Denby Dale*

PHOTOCOPIER
noises made: *Brampton Bierlow*

POSTURE
determinedly heterosexual effeminate: *Campsall*

PREGNANT
feeling bump: *Ogden*

PUBS
being served: *Noblethorpe*
hand dryer moisture: *Ousethorpe*
ironic groan: *Wawne*
"dead" drinks: *Yarm*

Q

QUEUE
jumper: *Scampston*
old lady: *Thirtleby*

R

RETORT
  too late: *Aston*

ROYAL CORRESPONDENTS
  smug expression: *Beamsley*

S

SALIVA
  released accidentally: *Burton Fleming*

SCHOOL
  enemy: *Old Edlington*
  bully's sidekick: *Midgley*
  boys on bus: Ugthorpe

SECRETS
  strange look: *Pontefract*
  impossible to keep: *Scissett*

SEX
  innuendo: *Ainderby Quernhow*
  foreplay: *Cullingworth*
  brushing teeth: *Methley*
  TV scene: *Ryther cum Ossendyke*

SHAVING
  missed bits: *Altofts*

SHOES
  grit in tread of: *Crigglestone*
  trying on: *Ulrome*

SHOPPING
  walking against arrows in Ikea: *Cowling*
  Item to distract: *Haxby*
  regret on missing sale: *Orgreave*
  leaving gift shop: *Skirpenbeck*

SHOPPING TROLLEY
  wonky: *Rolston*

SHOWERS
  hot, cold: *Scalby*

SINGING
  pretending: *Thwing*

SMOKE
  avoiding: *Ulley*

SMOKERS
  outside: *Hackenthorpe*

SNOOKER
  lucky pot: *Spaunton*
  cool indifference: *Swinden*

SOCIAL OCCASION
  backing out of: *Todwick*

SPOTS
  mutated: *Great Ouseburn*
  ugly: *Grimston*
  too much concealer: *Pockley*

STAIRS
  stumble down: *Boulderclough*
  extra step at bottom: *Follifoot*
  landing: *Luddendenfoot*
  stumbling on landing: *Lund*

STICKY TAPE
no starting point: *Riddlesden*

STOOLS
relatively solid: *Midhopestones*
next stage from Midhopestones:
Dropping-well

STORAGE
no category: *Hardraw*

STRANGERS
distance from city: *Sancton*

STUBBORN
refusing to put something
down: *Balk*

STUDENTS
traffic cones: *Skeffling*
microwave: *Upper Poppleton*

SUPERMARKETS
socially awkward: *Ellerker*
cashier not looking at PIN:
High *Gardham*
free samples: *Pinchinthorpe*
old lady queuing: *thirtleby*
bag: *Wressle*

T

TEA
To make in emergency:
Kettlewell

TECHNOLOGY
hatred of: *Aukley*

TELEVISION
button on remote: *Adby*
watching too much: *Drub*
presenters' chemistry:
Hoylandswaine
sex awkwardness: *Ryther cum
Ossendyke*

TEXTING
sent to wrong person: *Blaxton*
predictive text gone wrong:
Copt Hewick
refusing to call: *Long Preston*
ex: *Yearsley*

THOUGHT
devoid of: *Gleadless*

TIME
setting fast: *Tockwith*
after tomorrow: *Whenby*
after Whenby: *Wensley*

TIPPING
hanging around: *Skeeby*

TISSUE
bedroom floor: *Tosside*

TOENAIL
gouge: *Skerne*

TOILET
left in unpleasant state: *Barnby
Dunn*
visiting to avoid work:
Dungworth
roll direction: *Haisthorpe*
seat: *Hinderwell*
Reading-material: *Micklebring*

using in relationship:
Moulton End
choosing public: *Piccadilly*
something left: *Skidby*
one eye shut: *Slaithwaite*
urinating: *Timble*

TOOLS
borrowing: *Borrowby*

TRAFFIC CONES
drunk students: *Skeffling*

TRAINS
glaring at strangers with colds:
Crossflatts
waiting on platform: *Gembling*
ghost: *Houlsyke*

TRAVEL
concern over packing: *Fitling*

TYPING
fast-paced spurt: *Claxton*

U

URINALS
standing too close: *Silpho*

V

VACUUMING
immune to: *Linthwaite*

W

WHEELIE BIN
using neighbour's: *Halsham*
Bottle bank noise: *Hellaby*

WHISTLING
too loudly: *Constable Burton*

WINDOWSILL
bending to see: *Nunkeeling*

WINE
mesh: *Metham*

WINKER
indiscriminate: *Thornton
Watlass*

WOODEN FLOORS
scratched: *Cragg Vale*
grit that scratches: *Crigglestone*

WORK
toilet to avoid: *Dungworth*
charm to avoid: *Lazenby*

WRITING
on hand: *Hanlith*
unclearly when can't spell:
Ruswarp

GREAT·N·ORTHERN
www.greatnorthernbooks.co.uk
@gnbooks